Peter Tully's
PICTURES of PAI[GNTON]
Part II

Other Obelisk Publications

ACKNOWLEDGEMENT: *I wish to thank all the kind friends, known and unknown, who have given, or loaned, me the photos reproduced herein., with particular thanks to Devon Library Services for their help and encouragement.*

First Published in 1992 by Obelisk Publications
2 Church Hill, Pinhoe, Exeter, Devon
Printed in Great Britain by Penwell Print Ltd, Callington, Cornwall

Title Page — A view of archery being played in Queen's Park in 1905 as seen from the railway embankment. The grandstand was destroyed by fire in the late 1970s and has since been redesigned and rebuilt. The trees in the foreground are now fully grown and some 50 feet high. The benches alongside the targets are for spectators who accompany the archers from end to end.

PAIGNTON.

H·561

This aerial view was probably taken in the late 1920s. Waterside Road and Camp are in the foreground, whilst Goodrington is in the middle distance. The Waterside Hotel and shops opposite have yet to be built. Louville is still an active camping ground and Clennon Valley is still just a marsh. Preston Down Road and the Duchy Drive area are still fields in the top left background. Paignton Pier can also be clearly recognised, whilst Preston is in the distance.

One of the earliest GWR buses for the Paignton to Totnes service was inaugurated 17th April 1905. Here it is photographed outside the Gerston Hotel in Station Square. In bad weather it surely must have been a most unpleasant journey for those sitting outside.

This nostalgic photo shows the Torbay Express (Paignton to Paddington 3 hrs 54 mins in 1924) on the Up line at Paignton Station, probably in the 1950s, hauled by the Upton Castle. During its lifetime this famous train brought thousands of holiday makers to Paignton. At 11.48 a.m. every weekday, dead on time, the powerful engines would pound their way up the line, the driver acknowledging a wave from Paignton North Box, seen off by a proud Stationmaster. How times have changed — but then nostalgia is an expensive luxury.

Here we see Paignton Station's Up platform, prior to the laying of the double track to Torquay (1910). The Booking Office was much nearer to the level crossing then, but moved up to this side of the bookstall just before the First World War. Much of the original station remains today. Note the child's three-wheeled pram and the tremendous amount of luggage on the porter's truck.

This is Broadsands in the late 1920s with hardly a building in sight, save for a few in Bascombe Road in the background. Staverton's Broadsands Estate and The Elbury Estate and car park developments have yet to be conceived. In those days there was far more countryside surrounding this southern end of Tor Bay.

GOODRINGTON RETREAT
PAIGNTON

107 Bellinger Paignton

This is the retreat at the southern end of Goodrington beaches. A limestone retaining wall around a small grassy area kept out most of the sea except in an easterly gale and refreshments were served within its confines. There was no promenade, just the glorious sands. A motor launch provided the easiest, and probably the fastest, way back to Paignton Harbour.

The construction of the Cliff Walk at Goodrington commenced in 1929 using government-sponsored labour from the depressed mining areas of South Wales. The lower promenade was built first, the ascending paths and Horseshoe then added. For some years this tourist (and local) attraction was unconnected with Goodrington Sea Front. Herbert Whitley of Paignton Zoo donated the majority of the trees, shrubs and palms.

The photo opposite shows the token tree planting ceremony in 1933 watched by a comparatively small group of onlookers (qv Book I p. 42). The temporary railway has been dismantled and the gardens look bare compared to their appearance today.

From construction to destruction — in February 1915 a portion of Paris Singer's wall at Preston was washed away. He was approached to rebuild it but declined and to this day there is a gap, roughly opposite Manor Road. This picture, which was taken about 1916, shows the boulders strewn about the beach. A few tents are scattered on Preston Green, but of particular interest is the clear picture of the Up and Down platforms at Preston Halt. The first mention of this minor railway stopping place was in the Paignton Observer in 1912, but it was closed in September 1914. Its position behind what is now Marine Parade is remembered only by a few items of railway memorabilia on a house in Orient Road. A number of these small halts were created on this line in the days when the railways' main aim, apart from making money for their investors, was to serve the public. Another, known as Broadsands Halt, opened in July 1928 and closed in 1929 — its actual whereabouts is unknown to me.

Opposite is an aerial photo of Paignton Sea Front in 1936. The Silver Jubilee arch of '35 is still standing. The Summer Pavilion replaced the circular bandstand, even though its tent remains. The Torbay Hotel at the bottom of Torbay Road became Page Johnson House. The whole of the foreground is now occupied by the Festival Theatre which was built in 1966. The last building on the right was Dellers Summer Cafe, now the Fiesta. Note the large open space (top left) now the site of the multi-storey car park and the Victoria Shopping Centre.

PAIGNTON
FROM THE AIR.

The Harbour

Above is a close-up view of the Paignton Club at Paignton Harbour (qv Book I p. 36) which was built in 1882, and is almost unchanged in its appearance today. The building to the right is Kingswood, at one time belonging to Paris Singer. He sent his wife to live there whilst entertaining Isadora Duncan at Oldway. Cllr Spanton occupied the property in the 1930s and 40s and was followed by his son-in-law, Jimmy Gillett. Pulled down in the 1980s, the site is now occupied by the aptly named Kingswood Court, a block of flats. Above left shows another part of Paignton Harbour which was built in 1838, and acquired by the PUDC in 1936. They appointed Miss Stella Gale as the first and only woman Harbourmaster in England. She later married John Holmes and ran the Chandlery on the South Quay. A trading schooner, similar to the one pictured, brought coal, timber and cement to Paignton. When it left it took away cargoes of cider, and the famous Paignton Flatpole cabbages. On the port bow of the topsail schooner, laying alongside, can be seen part of the twin hulls of one of the first catamarans to be sailed in Tor Bay. This picture was probably taken about 1890.

Left is a view of Paignton Harbour, possibly taken in the 1920s. The Harbour Light Cafe was still a boat store, and the coast guard station was still in use. Before the installation of the trot mooring chains in the late 1940s, boats were moored haphazardly by attaching chains to heavy weights buried in the sand or to the cross pieces of wood in the foreground which were buried in the harbour bottom.

The Paignton coastline has witnessed some dramatic shipwrecks notably during easterly gales. Left is the German Torpedo Boat-Destroyer S24 which ran aground off Roundham Head on the night of 13th December 1920. She was being pulled by a tug called Warrior from Cherbourg to Teignmouth in order to be scrapped. However she went adrift and met her fate in Tor Bay. Bailey and Bradshaw landed a sizable salvage job.

The bottom two photos show the shipwreck of River Lagan some four years later. Built in Glasgow in 1882 she was on passage from Portsmouth around to Swansea but went aground at Goodrington. She survived the ordeal but in 1927 became a total wreck hitting Skerry Vore Rock when bound from Stornaway to Hamburg.

Shown here is one of the few photographs in existence of the west side of the Gerston Hotel showing the entrance to the Royal Bijou Theatre, which was created by the amateur Thespian, Hyde Dendy. It was here that The Pirates of Penzance was first performed on 30th December 1879. Until its demolition a few years ago, the rear entrance to the hotel was still the arch just to the left of the horse. This view would have been impossible to take today because Hyde Road shops were built immediately opposite.

This sharp photo shows The Hydro Hotel in Esplanade Road, and was taken about 1930. It is now known as the Esplanade Hotel. Originally a terrace of private houses, the southernmost was at one time a nursing home (during the First World War) but was later turned into the mock Tudor edifice shown here, the owners having acquired the adjoining three properties. It became the Esplanade when the original Esplanade (built by Hyde Dendy) was renamed, firstly as the Prince Regent and today as the Inn on the Green.

Above is a view of Paignton Sea Front probably in the late 1920s or early 30s when we had a Home Fleet to visit Torbay. The general air of clutter — posts, lamp standards, flag poles, railings — would be frowned on today. However we are now unable to recreate that sense of unhurried enjoyment captured in this photograph. The band in the tent provided background music to those unable to afford the 6d to go inside. Other enjoyments included a gentle stroll, sitting on the Monkey Rack, or just a leisurely evening spent at the seaside. The Entertainments Manager, Harold Bultz, had his office in the hut by the central gardens.

The wooden latticed arch was constructed at the bottom of Torbay Road to celebrate the Silver Jubilee of King George V and Queen Mary in 1935. It was illuminated by hundreds of bulbs installed by the Paignton Electric Light Company under the supervision of Mr Johnson. The arch remained as a tourist attraction until 1936 when the King died, as it was thought inappropriate for it to remain.

The Esplanade, Paignton. 951.

Paignton Sea Front, just after the First World War, was a busy place with bath chairs, ice-cream carts, horse drawn vans and bicycles being challenged by a solitary motor car. The first shelters were erected in 1892 the year after the Great Blizzard.

From 1866 regulations forbade men and women swimming together. Men had to use Preston beach, whilst women had to use Paignton. This meant that Hyde-Dendy, owner of the pier, steamboat and bathing machines, got no male custom! However, attitudes gradually changed and mixed bathing was eventually allowed. Dendy finally sold his 30 machines, office and equipment to the PUDC for £1,425 in 1920. They were removed in 1925.

Park House School, Lower Polsham Road, was one of the two major private schools for boys in the early part of this century, catering primarily for boarders. The site of the school building, now demolished, is at present occupied by Oldenburg Place. The school was started by a Mr Gilbert in 1908 at Parkhill House, Southfield Road; he remained as headmaster until 1931. In 1910 the school moved to two houses in Adelphi Terrace, christened "Park House", before moving to the Polsham Road building after the First World War. The Redcliffe Hotel, shown here as it appeared in 1904, was built for a Col. Robert Smith. It was begun in 1855 by a Paignton builder, Mr

Tozer, and was completed in 1865, sited on 5.5 acres of land and foreshore. "Redcliffe Tower", as it was known, was approached through entrance gates with a domed hexagonal lodge. These were pulled down when Marine Drive was constructed.

A storm in 1867 swept away a hydropathic plunge bath on the seaward side of the building. It was connected to the house by a subway and filled with sea water at every high tide. Smith died in 1873 and the house was sold by his son. Eventually it was bought by Paris Singer (1877), who developed the surrounding land, built Preston sea wall (qv Book I p. 28) and sold the first building plot to Robert Waycott. The latter built Villa Marina which was later converted into a convalescent home for the South African war wounded. Redcliffe was sold by Singer in 1902, when it became a hotel, and was extensively altered.

"The Pavilion Pier was opened in June 1879. It was erected solely by and under the personal superintendence of Mr Dendy of Paignton and his foreman, Mr Richard Harris, for the Paignton Pier Company, incorporated by Act of Parliament, 37th and 38th Vict., c.47. In 1881 the Pier-head was enlarged and the Billiard Room (36 feet by 28 feet) built in connection with the Pavilion. The length of the Pier is 780 feet (including the Pier-head 140 feet by 54 feet). The Pavilion measures 80 feet by 25 feet, and is connected with another Refreshment Room and a Billiard Room, which has two tables by "Thurston and Co." It is elegantly decorated, brilliantly lighted, and fitted-up with a moveable stage. It also boasts a Grand Organ, Harmonium, Grand Piano, Kettle-drums, and other instruments. Musical performances take place in the Pavilion two or three times a day in the season, and Organ Recitals of sacred music are given on Sunday afternoons and at other times. Gilbert and Sullivan's comic opera *Pinafore*, under the title of *HMS Pinafore on the Water* was played here by Mr D'Oyley Carte's full company on 27th and 28th July 1880. Rinking is practised on the body of the Pier and Bathing from the Pier-head is permitted up to eight a.m." *Quote taken from "Paignton and its Attractions 1885", written by Dendy himself.*

Opposite we see the healthy and hardy young members who participated in Paignton Amateur Swimming Club's opening dip on 20th May 1911. The photo was taken on Paignton Pier and reveals a wide range of expressions.

Dogs chased stones in 1900 just as they do today! This is a fine picture of the Pier Pavilion taken before it was burnt down in 1919.

The scene above was probably photographed in the 1920s after the pier fire when an attempt had been made to cover in the entire length, I suspect with corrugated iron. Today the cost of the flags alone would be astronomical. With the apparently 'fixed' sides at the seaward end of the pier, all the side seating had been lost.

This shot was probably taken in the same year but on a sunny day. It shows the shore end of Dendy's pier with the four original kiosks complete with their pointed roofs. Compared with today's beach wear, the people seem very overdressed. The little boys wore their sailor suits with pride.

This shows the top of Cecil Road where it linked up with Southfield Road. There was less than 10 feet of width between the cobbled pavements. The buildings on the right were demolished and the present Cecil Road Council Depot was constructed here.

This architectural gem is the Marist Convent School in Fisher Street, photographed about 1920. It was built by Henry John Bailey in 1890. He also gave us the Tropicana in Station Square, the Pot Black Club in Winner Street and Coniston in Sands Road. The house was sold to the Marist Sisters early in 1908 when they moved from what became the Goodrington Hotel and Quay West. The school was enlarged during the 1930s and a dormitory block built behind and to the left. It closed in 1982 when the Marist Sisters moved to a private house in Preston. The property was sold and re-opened as the Tower House School (qv p.26).

Paignton has something of a reputation for grand celebrations, a good example being these 1935 Silver Jubilee celebrations in Church Street (shown opposite). Some sort of procession is wending its way from Winner Street down to the parish church of St John the Baptist. The good natured crowd needed only two policemen to clear a way for what must have been a makeshift band. There appears to be few men in the procession so could it have been the Mothers Union?

The sign above the door tells us that this is Chard Bros store in Winner Street. Established in 1844 as Dellers, it was the forerunner of others in Palace Avenue, Torbay Road and Seaway Corner. Lambshead, who owned the firm, sold out in 1926 to concentrate on his empire in Torbay Road. The main store became the one in Palace Avenue. I imagine a gas light was attached to the swan's neck pipe in winter time when the sun blinds would be removed.

Dellers Supply Stores were built by Lambshead to supplement his existing store in Winner Street. With Couldrey and Bridgman he was also responsible for the purchase and development of Palace Avenue. Later he moved 'down town' to build Queen's Park Mansions and then Dellers Cafe (qv Book I pp 20/21). In the 1920s Dellers Stores (all four branches) were bought by Chard Bros. After the Second World War they sold the premises in this photograph to Rossiters who own it today and run it as Paignton's largest department store.

Bailey's Hotel in Station Square was built in 1894. At different times it has housed various businesses, Nick's repository, the Constitutional Club, Tropicana, Images, Ritzy's and finally, Kirsty's.

Emmanuel Beare's shop at 18—20 Victoria Street, Paignton was built in 1890. On the top floor were A.C. Howard & Wood, solicitors prior to their move to chambers above Lloyds Bank in Palace Avenue. The shop was sold in the middle of this century to become Liptons, and then later a discount chemist which didn't survive for very long. It is now "Iceland", the frozen food firm. The reverse reflection in the window is of Rose and Harvey's ladies lingerie shop now occupied by the Nat. West Bank. Howard & Wood's offices have now gone a full circle and are the home of Courtney Richards & Company solicitors, formed by the amalgamation of Courtney Rallison and Stanley Richards, who at one time occupied chambers over the Nat. West Bank.

This was the new Paignton Co-operative Society shop in Winner Street built, as the iron letters show, in 1906. The multiplicity of large gas lamps must have cast a brilliant glow to the pavements prior to street lighting. The pillars and rails on the pavements edge support the summer sun blinds. Interest at the savings bank (open every Saturday from 2 to 5 p.m.) was 3.5% per annum (who would have any money to save after the week-end anyhow?)

An Italian, Joseph Valley, came to Torquay at the end of the 19th century but died soon afterwards in 1903. His son, another Joseph, with his French wife started an Ice-cream business in Market Street, Torquay. Our pictures show the ice-cream being manufactured. A fleet of hand and horse-drawn carts distributed the finished product around the town and seafront. They opened a shop in Union Street, Torquay and another in Victoria Street, Paignton. Both shops were renowned for their yellow canaries and marble topped tables at which one devoured delicious ice cream sundaes. Their magnificent displays of chocolates and sweets did particularly well at Christmas time.

The photograph was taken on the occasion of the annual outing of employees and management of L.A. Langler & Son, builders and decorators of 27 Winner Street. It was taken in 1906, and every man sported some form of headwear!
Front row: Head, Madge, Pople, Whiteway; Second row: Helson, J. Langler, C. Langler, Holmes, Farrant, Perryman, Maunder; Third row: Perrett, Kerslake, Mudge, Ekers, Parnell; Back row: Madge, White, Holmes, Whiteway.

This beautifully set up picture is taken at the annual outing of employees and management of Starkey, Knight and Ford, the Brewers, of Princess Street. Looking altogether more cheerful than those celebrating opposite — it was perhaps the result of sampling some of the firm's wares before the photo was taken!

A serious fire on the 20th June 1927 destroyed these thatched cottages adjoining the Globe Inn in Winner Street. Despite the presence of the Paignton Fire Brigade, many onlookers were enlisted to help, presumably to hold the hose! There seemed to be no shortage of assistance to remove the furniture from the pub in case the fire should spread. Can you imagine the general public being allowed anywhere near such a blaze today?

The new Shand Mason horse-drawn steam fire engine was bought for the Paignton Fire Brigade in 1907 at a cost of £348, a large sum at the time. It replaced the old manual pumping machine which required much labour to provide pressure to the hoses. The Shand Mason machine was still pulled by the two horses which were kept to pull the local dustcart! When the fire 'hooter' was sounded, the driver of the cart would unhook the horses, wherever he was, and ride them pell-mell back to the fire station behind the public hall (built in 1890). The first man to arrive at the station would light the steam boiler in order to get pressure to the pumps. The whole entourage would then set off to the scene of the fire — trusting that the fire had not yet burnt itself out.

This is how Waycott's Corner looked on the morning of July 5th 1952. The fire started at the head of the stairs on the first floor in rooms occupied by Peter Bessell, later Liberal MP for Bodmin. Flames soon spread through exploding gas mains to Brounettes Gown Shop, Purdy's tobacconist shop and up Victoria Street to engulf the floors above Maynards. The building was gutted and most of the premises below suffered serious water damage. The walls which were left standing were pulled down later in the day. The premises are now occupied by Wilkins & Partners.

Above left we have the ladies of the Paignton ARP (Air Raid Precaution) taken about 1941. Standing L to R: Mrs Hodgson, Mrs Hooper, Mrs Bill Coysh, Mrs Harold Bultz. Seated L to R: Mrs McGinity, Mrs Chidgey, Mrs Hicks.

The 'matching pair' features several of the 'other halves' who were Second World War ARP leaders, later known as Civil Defence (Torbay). Judging by the long service strips this photograph must have been taken in 1942 or 43. Included in the picture is Deputy Surveyor W. Chidgey, Town Clerk Sam Hodgson and Entertainments Manager Harold Bultz.

These are the ladies of Paignton's Auxiliary Fire Service who served during the Second World War. Amongst those here are the two Battershall sisters Vera and Mottie, Mary Rowe, Sadie Grant and Pauline Taylor.

This is Kirkham Cottage between Colley End Road and Littlegate Road photographed in the early 1930s. It clearly shows the Paignton gas holder in Churchward Road. The site is now occupied by the Council's Cecil Road Depot and Tor Work Social Club. The wall on the left belonged to Effords the large house which would now, had it not been pulled down, have stood right in the middle of Cecil Road. Access from Colley End Road and the cemetery to Torquay Road could only be obtained by turning left at Effords into Southfield Road, going past Beesley's Furniture Depository (at one time belonging to Manning Williams) bearing right at the Methodist Chapel and joining up with the top end of Cecil Road.

This photograph, taken in June 1901, shows Coverdale Tower and part of the wall of the Bishop's Palace. Originally the manor of Peintone belonged to the Bishops of Exeter. Bishop Osbern built the tower and protecting wall in 1072. The property passed from the control of the church in 1557 to the Earl of Pembroke. The local board, a forerunner of PUDC, were offered the tower and adjoining Palace Orchard for £750 which they turned down. It was bought instead by the Rev. A. Linzee Giles (vicar 1908—1914) and given to the 'living'. The villas on the right were built to house the engineers responsible for the construction of the Torbay and Dartmouth railway to Paignton in 1859. The house shown here is now a Doctor's Surgery.

This street party took place in Palace Place to celebrate the Coronation of Queen Elizabeth II in May 1953. Reverend and Mrs Pedley are seen on the right whilst some of the crowd sport some distinctive masks.

This photograph was taken at the Paignton Amateur Operatic Society's production of Iolanthe *at the Palace Avenue Theatre in 1955. With Geoffrey Snelson as Producer and John Hopwood as musical director, the cast included Dora Deller, Ron & Mary Wellens, Joe Finch, Phyllis and Norman Elliot, Godfrey Farrant, Pat and Donald Wood, Molly Joiner, Gertrude Wyatt, Esme Vowles, Dennis Isles, Bert Davey, Ernie Campion, Cliff Pritchard, Gloria Watkins, Ken and Doris Rowe, June Williams, Vera Whiting and Charlie Patterson. It featured Bill Coysh as the Chancellor, Pauline Norris as Phyllis, Jack Sanders as Private Willis, Marjorie Marriott as the Fairy Queen and Alice Down as Iolanthe.*

Shown here are most of the Masters and some of the boys at Tweenaway Secondary School in 1958. There are many old familiar faces in the group! The school was built by Paignton builder Dick Peeke, whose his son Bruce once ran the London Inn in Church Street.

Before the absorption of the PUDC with Brixham UDC and Torquay TC to create the County Borough of Torbay in September 1967, it was customary for an annual dinner of Paignton Councillors and employees and their wives to be held at Oldway. Among those on the stairs are Mr and Mrs Shilston Sharp, Mr and Mrs Sam Hodgson, Mr and Mrs George Stabb, Major and Mrs Bentley, Mr and Mrs Les Hicks, Mr and Mrs Craze, Mr and Mrs Spanton, Mrs Flemons, Messrs. Batteshall, Peters, Thick and Matthews. Mr Rex Sercombe is perched on the balcony. This photograph was taken in 1948 or 1949.

This photograph of the PUDC platoon of 10th Devon (Torbay) Home Guard was taken in front of the corrugated shelter in Queen's Park about 1943. Among the group were: fourth from left in the front row, Kintersbeare, Parks Inspector; third from left in the back row, Gilbert Hallett; second from left in the middle row, George Lovatt. The owner and name of the dog remains unknown!

The pristine group are the Young Helpers League photographed at Primley House in about 1906. The lady in black (fourth from right in the second row down) is Mrs Eleanor Whitley, widow of Edward Whitley, Lord Mayor of Liverpool and brewery baron of that city. She was the mother of Herbert plus three other sons. She arrived in Paignton in 1904. The young man second from the left in the second row back was Arthur Came, with his sister just in front of him, whilst the girl on his left is Mrs Dixon of Lower Blagdon.

Paignton St Michael's AFC season 1926—27 was a successful one as they were winners of the Torbay Herald Football Challenge Cup. Back row, L to R: C. Roberts (President), E. Bell, N. Gray, G. Durbin, Bert Yeoman, J. Narracott, H. Parnell; Middle row: W. Foley, Percy Foster, Len Pawley, W. Cross, Bill Wood, G. Harwood; Front row: P. Bovey, Tom Stoneman (captain), Jack Langmead

An exhibition organised by the Torquay and Paignton Gas Light and Coke Company, held in Dellers summer ballroom in 1936, attracted quite a gathering of ladies. Billed as 'Comforts Biggest Bargains', the show extolled the benefits of gas cooking, heating and refrigeration. The first two still hold good, but production has ceased of gas fridges.

This serious group are members of the Rotary Club of Paignton, seen here photographed in 1941, some 15 years after its charter. They are lunching at Dellers Cafe in the upper ballroom. In 1963 when the cafe was demolished (qv Book I p. 21) the club moved to the Harbour Light Restaurant and still meets there every Thursday at 1.00 p.m. Among these early war-time members are: President E. R. Hooper, F. L. Green, T. Mitchell-Fox, Jasper Evans, Frank, Harris, John Sutton, Rev. Montague Dale, Jack Eastley, L. B. Griffin, T. Vickery, R. T. Letcher, H. H. Fielding, Roland Foster, W. H. Webber, G. Ireland, Doctor Campbell, Carter Ellis and Hunter-Joy.

This is Torbay Road at Preston, looking down towards Seaway Corner, taken from outside the tram depot, now Lathams Car Sales. In this photo there is only one shop on the left hand side — now, of course,they are all shops! The newspaper shop opposite, at the bottom of Fortescue Road is still there but in 1912 there was no Lloyds Bank, no traffic lights and only gas street lighting.

To finish our second nostalgic look at Paignton, overleaf we have an aerial view of Torquay and Paignton Gas Light and Coke Company's Hollacombe Works. Built in 1861, it survived more than a century until it closed in 1968. In 1879 the town had 110 gas street lamps and in 1904 the company gave the town 200 of the new Incandescent lamps. This photo was probably taken in 1930, soon after the completion of the new large gas holder. To the right of it is Roundhill Road (no shops) and joining that is Cockington Lane. At this time it was only a narrow tree-covered track crossing the stream by a ford. Prior to the building of the Torquay to Paignton main road, as we know it, this lane connected Preston with Torquay via the narrow one-way lane at the end of Langdon Road. It cut through what is now Broadley Drive, and dropped down into Cockington Village behind the Eastern Lodge.